# God is Anonymous, Too

## Taoist Threads in Twelve-Step Recovery

By Joseph E. Galligan

FOR LINDA,
LOVE JOE
6/30/16

"Cheaters, liars, outlaws and fallen angels
come looking for the grace from which they fell."
from *"Camelot Motel"*
by Mary Gauthier


"Whichever way your pleasure tends,
if you plant ice, you're gonna harvest wind."
from *"Franklin's Tower"*
by Jerry Garcia and Robert Hunter

# TABLE OF CONTENTS

# Introduction

Many people in 12-Step programs struggle with the word "God" in the Twelve Steps because to them that word equates to the hypocrisy and rule-mongering of the religions in which they were raised as children.

Perhaps you have heard this before: "Religion is for people who don't want to go to Hell. Spirituality in 12-Step programs is for people who have been to Hell and don't want to go back."

If this book helps you see that you cannot progress in 12-Step recovery without belief in a power merely *other* than yourself, never mind *greater* than yourself, then it has served its purpose.

While the book should serve its greatest purpose to those recovering from addiction, it may also have meaning to those using the Twelve Steps to deal with other life-threatening issues, such as loving a person active in his or her addiction. The generic term "addict" is generally used here because what is called an "alcoholic" is really someone who is addicted to a drug called ethanol, the active ingredient in beer, wine and hard liquor.

I am a recovering addict/alcoholic, and I am a grateful member of a 12-Step program. But this book is not "about Alcoholics Anonymous" because no one speaks for AA; it is actually a virtual organization. To paraphrase an old Buddhist saying, if you see the spokesman for AA on the street, kill him. AA is merely *one* place where 12-Step recovery happens. So are Narcotics Anonymous and the myriad other programs based on the Twelve Steps. This book tries to avoid the AA/NA term "sponsor," preferring the much more inclusive term "teacher." In the book *Alcoholics Anonymous* (the so-called "Big Book") the term is "trusted friend."

My poems (printed in italics in the first three sections and which comprise the section "The Student and His Teacher") reflect an experience shaped by AA/NA, and so do the prose commentaries throughout, but: one can find spiritual relief and guidance in any kind of fellowship. *The point for anyone recovering from addiction or its effects is to avoid isolation and secrecy.* In its simplest terms, the spirituality talked about in 12-Step programs is based on gaining a sense of belonging and losing the sense of isolation that dogs every active addict or codependent. It is about connecting to something positive outside yourself that has the power to offset all the negativity and self-loathing inside yourself.

In my own case, I knew right away—in my first week at a treatment center at age 49—that recovery offered a sense of belonging that I had only found, strangely enough, on a softball team once. As I entered recovery back in my life at home, that sense of belonging became even stronger. But it wasn't until I read a book called *The Tao of Physics*, by Fritjof Capra, that I saw spirituality in 12-Step recovery has nothing to do with the God I learned about in the Episcopal Church and everything to do with a simple concept of "goodness" or "rightness." I never *felt* the meaning of what people call "God" until I read that book.

Capra points out that the people working on the far edges of astrophysics and molecular biology find that the more they learn, the more mysterious their subject matter grows. He finds this phenomenon parallel to that of the sages in Eastern religions. These sages learned that the most fundamental truth is at once extremely simple and yet complicated beyond all human comprehension. The more you know, the less you understand. The less you understand, the less you need to know. Paradox is everything. A trust in a simple truth or underlying rightness of things is crucial in 12-Step recovery. There is no need to define a "Higher Power," only to have one in whatever form it may take. The authors of the Big Book appeared to address this issue with the phrase " ... God, as we understood Him." Unfortunately, the capital-him created a number of roadblocks for those who preferred a her or it or them approach to a higher power. The problem became to read around "God" and "Him" to find the spiritual essence of the book, not take issue with some of its individual words. Shakespeare is full of words we find offensive today, but we don't rewrite *Hamlet* or *Macbeth* in order to make it more palatable to a 21st-century audience.

Capra mentions the Zen concept of "original face" ( p. 36), and my immediate reaction to that was, "That's the Second Step!" (see p. 39) My problem with that step at first was not, "Am I insane?" but rather, "When was I ever sane?" Through Capra and subsequent explorations that led me to study Taoism, I came to understand that the sanity promised in the Second Step is found by:

- don't drink or do drugs no matter what today

- get out of my own way

- let things come to me

- remember that what goes around comes around

- resist the urge to put everything into cognitive classifications

- believe that I must hold at bay the power of an inner voice that wants to get me alone and kill me

- feel or sense, not *imagine*, my rightful sense of place in the world

- know that I have an inherent purity of spirit

- understand and accept the pain of the innocence I lost

- ask for restoration of the grace from which I fell

- work Steps 3 through 11 to arrive at the promise of Step 12 — "Having had a spiritual awakening as a result of these steps ..."

Long before most of us became addicts, we fell from God's grace (or out of the Tao), and as the singer Mary Gauthier puts it, "That's a long way to fall." But no addict has fallen so far that they can't find grace again. Not as long as one's still breathing.

The two Taoist texts quoted here are *The Complete I Ching*, by Alfred Huang, and *Tao Te Ching*, by Lao Tzu (translated by Man-Ho Kwok, Martin Palmer and Jay Ramsay). The intent of this book is not to "sell" Taoism (to do so is totally *not* Tao anyway) or offer it as the only non-Christian or non-Western way to fill the spiritual void that is common to every addict. It's just another way to see, another pathway to feeling, another door to belonging. If the religion you were raised in does that for you in recovery, good for you. This book is for people who find that not to be true.

Tao is translated in English as "the Way." The proclamation of Jesus — "I am the way" — can be written: "I am Tao." Whether you believe Jesus was the son of God or a revolutionary prophet is irrelevant in this view. A man by that name who arose out of Nazareth 21 centuries ago manifested Tao in everything he did and said. The religion this prophet/deity gave rise to in the 100 years following his death is what the founders of Alcoholics Anonymous were striving to return to.

The moral philosophy of Taoism fits 12-Step recovery because it allows for the existence of all deities, all faiths, all creation myths, all people. The Judeo-Christian "God" or "Yaweh" is one very powerful manifestation of Tao. A sense of inclusion, of connection to goodness, is what every active addict is missing and what he or she must regain in order to stay clean and sober. The beauty of 12-Step programs is we can call the force that creates this sense of inclusion anything we want. The word "anonymous" literally means "having no name." The fact that even "God" is anonymous in 12-Step programs falls into line with the first chapter of *Tao Te Ching*, (p.27), which says:

"The Tao that can be talked about is not the true Tao.
The name that can be named is not the eternal Name."

Tao is what Jesus, Buddha, Mohammed, Shiva and Raven all sprang from. It's what all of us sprang from, and it's what we will all return to. Taoism also requires active involvement from mankind to manage the dynamic interaction between *yin* and *yang* (see glossary) to its maximum benefit. The parallel here to the 12-Step philosophy is striking. "God" will do for us what we couldn't do for ourselves (quit drinking or using other drugs, basically), but this force requires us to take further action once that fundamental barrier to goodness (God-ness) is removed (the obsession of the mind). All *yang* is no good; it's overwhelming. All *yin* is no good, either; nothing gets done. It takes action to create the proper blend of *yin* and *yang* in accordance with the current situation. No one just hands you the ability to achieve balance in your life, which is what people who never get past Step Three in 12-Step recovery discover.

We cannot take the Second Step unless we believe that something outside of ourselves can end the insanity that comes with "I won't let myself get drunk this time" or "If I could just get the kids to stop bugging him, he won't use drugs any more" or "I'll just make one more bet to get even." In the Third Step we only trust this goodness with our thoughts ("will') and actions ("life"). Then there are nine more steps that require willingness and then action on our part. Without that action, we will be dragged by our own minds back into that non-Tao place we came from, except this time it will be worse. For me, being dragged back by my mind means I will die an ugly, lonely, pointless death and regain my soul-sickness and carry that sickness with me into what I believe will be my next life. For a person who loves an addict, being dragged back means even more of the insanity that comes from trying to extinguish the sun with a garden hose.

The book's format in the first three parts is quotations from the texts mentioned above, followed by small Tao-ish poems of mine related to that quotation's subject. In each of these sections are some related references to *Alcoholics Anonymous* (4th edition), and

*Twelve Steps and Twelve Traditions (1953).*

These discussions in some cases reflect my own experience with recovery because in some cases, that's all I can do—tell you what happened to me. The only aspect of "what I do" that is relevant to this book is 10 years as a chemical dependency counselor and clinical supervisor. Some of what I write about comes from that experience, but not a lot. The clinic only confirms what I see on the street and in the rooms of AA. I have as of this writing, according to a cell phone application, been clean and sober for 5,525 days, each one another miracle day, but my immediate problem is day 5,526. Put another way, I can say that's 5,525 yesterdays I haven't screwed up by getting loaded. I may have screwed up those yesterdays in other ways, but for a fact I haven't done it by getting loaded.

I contain the experience, strength and hope of all the people who have shared their lives with me in recovery.

The end of the book is a series of discourses between a "student and his teacher." Earlier, I talk about "sponsors" and "sponsees" (an ugly word that I wish there was a substitute for) but student and teacher are really what these relationships are about.

This book is best read read from front to back. It builds on itself. The Taoist quotes and poems require meditative reflection on the reader's part. The poems are dense condensations of original writing and a process of humility undertaken after someone told me, "You love your words too much." You might find something in these pages to help your own explorations of spirituality. You might use them to guide journaling. You might use them to connect your head to your heart.

*Tao Te Ching* ( p. 74) tells you that you are human and that:

"Humanity is schooled by Earth,
Earth is taught by Heaven,
And Heaven is guided by the Tao,
And the Tao
        goes with what is absolutely natural."

May the difference between your sobriety date and mine never change.

Joseph Edward Galligan
Portland Oregon

# THE TWELVE STEPS

1. We admitted that we were powerless over alcohol [and other drugs] – that our lives had become unmanageable.

2. Came to believe that a power greater than ourselves could restore us to sanity.

3. Made a decision to turn our will and our lives over to the care of God *as we understood Him.*

4. Made a searching and fearless moral inventory of ourselves.

5. Admitted to ourselves, to God and to another human being the exact nature of our wrongs.

6. Were entirely ready to have God remove all these defects of character.

7. Humbly asked Him to remove our shortcomings.

8. Made a list of all persons we had harmed and became willing to make amends to them all.

9. Made direct amends to such people wherever possible, except when to do so would injure them or others.

10. Continued to take personal inventory and when we were wrong promptly admitted it.

11. Sought through prayer and meditation to improve our conscious contact with God, praying only for the knowledge of His will for us and the power to carry it out.

12. Having had a spiritual awakening as the result of these steps, we tried to carry this message to alcoholics [addicts, codependents] and to practice these principles in all our affairs.

# TAOISM GLOSSARY

Ching: big (that is, holy) book. Taoists respect any *"ching,"* including the Bible and the Koran. To them, the "Big Book" of AA (called *Alcoholics Anonymous* and first published in 1939) is a literal translation of *"ching"* into English. *Tao Te Ching* means "The Holy Book of the Way and Virtue." That's not a bad alternative title for *Alcoholics Anonymous*.

I: change

Tao (pronounced "dow"): literally, "the way." Tao is not a being or a place; it is more like the resonating force of perfect balance.

Te: literally, "virtue." Virtue is best summarized in the 12-Step phrase, "do the next right thing."

Wu-wei: literally, "doing by not doing." A concept that encompasses the idea "let it come to you" or "don't just do something, sit there."

Yang: One of the two elemental energy forces in Taoism, it represents heaven, giving and aggression. Associated with the male.

Yao: One of the lines, either yin or yang, that make up the 64 hexagrams in *The I Ching*. Yin is represented by a broken line and yang by a solid line. Three *yao* make a *gua*, and two *gua* stacked together make the hexagrams. The eight primary *gua* are heaven, wind, water, mountain, earth, thunder, fire and lake.

Yin: One of the two elemental energy forces, it represents earth, receiving and passivity. Associated with the female.

# BEGINNINGS

"Alterations of the six yao unfold the truth;
Transformations of the opposites bring forth the feeling."

*The Complete I Ching*, page 31

## Beginnings – One

"Putting aside your spiritual tortoise.
Staring at me with mouth drooling.
Misfortune.

Staring at me with drooling mouth.
It is not a noble manner."

*The Complete I Ching*, page 234.

### Craving

*To crave poison
is to stroke nettles,
hug boiling water
or kiss leeches.*

*There is no why for this
only what.*

The Big Book is full of examples of how, left to their own devices, addicts persist in destroying themselves despite repeated earlier destructive encounters with their preferred vehicle for achieving oblivion.

"The idea that somehow, someday he will control and enjoy his drinking [or drug using] is the great obsession of every abnormal drinker [and addict]. The persistence of this illusion is astonishing. Many pursue it into the gates of insanity and death. (Big Book, p.30)

These three sentences, in my opinion, are the most important ones that occur back-to-back-to back in the Big Book. The first sentence has one crucial conjunctive word in it — "and." The fact is the conjunction should be "or." You can control it *or* you can enjoy it. You can't do both. If you find that you can, in fact, do both you are either not an addict (or "chemically dependent" in treatment-speak) or you haven't gotten there yet. The second sentence points to the fact that active addicts are walking around in an illusive world, and only they or other addicts believe it's real. The third sentence echoes the mantra of Narcotics Anonymous — do this or you will find that institutions, jails and death are your only reward.

There is no medical cure for this kind of insanity. No amount of "figuring it out" will help either. In 12-Step rooms around the world are slogans posted on the wall that seem at first to be so trite they make your teeth ache, but as I get to later, these slogans carry powerful truth. A slogan you will never see in a 12-Step meeting room is "Figure It Out!"

Addiction lives in our minds, not our bodies, as evidenced by the fact that there are people who cannot stop drinking alcohol once they start and then put down the alcohol for months or years and widely proclaim that it is seriously not OK for them to pick up a drink but then one day they do just that. There is no alcohol in their bodies when they do that. A distorted, illusive *idea* of alcohol is in their minds, however, and the mind tells the body to do something really stupid. So if we analyze our sick minds *with* our sick minds, we can expect only more sickness. As the Big Book (p. 85) puts it:

> "What we really have is a daily reprieve [from the insanity of our disease] contingent on the maintenance of our spiritual condition."

## Beginnings – Two

"If you mold a cup, you have to make it hollow;
it is the emptiness within that makes it useful."

*Tao Te Ching*, page 46

### Mansions of the Addicts

*The walls and roof
create shape.
The shape creates
usefulness.
People living
in the mansions
of addiction
don't use the space
because, though home,
they aren't there.*

Coming to believe that a power greater than ourselves will restore us to sanity means living life from the inside out. With alcohol, the prevailing wisdom is recovering addicts become healthier in their bodies after about 30 days and in their minds after about three months (thus the suggestion of 90 meetings in your first 90 days of recovery). But spiritual healing, the useful part over the long haul, comes from continuously emptying yourself out and achieving:

"… the personality change sufficient to bring about recovery from alcoholism [and other addictions]" (*Big Book*, p. 567).

As we empty out, we get rid of what hasn't been working and create useful space to add the things that are working. This is really what Steps Four and Five are all about.

Imagine that you are a block of wood, and recovery is water. Water poured over a block of wood runs off. Water poured into a block of wood that has been carved out is contained. We can't hold recovery unless we carve out addict thinking and behavior. And if we don't drink the recovery water and ask for more, water poured into the full cup will spill out, just like it did when we were drink- or drug-addled "blockheads."

Our "look good" is no good in a spiritual life. If we aren't using the interior space created by our recovery, then we are not changing. We are either working on our recovery or working on our relapse because our minds will fill the empty space with crap like "I don't need this anymore" and "One hit off that bong can't possibly cause any problems."

In some cases, 12-Step programs and people in them create a self-fulfilling prophecy of doom. And that is too much attention paid to how much time one has accrued in a 12-Step program. This only abets egotism and also makes it far more devastating when a person loses that time. A useful antidote to this false pride is, "The years are for us. The days are for me."

Recovery is one place where black and white thinking is helpful to the addict. There is nothing in between recovery and relapse. And the relapse *ends* with that first drink or drug. It's been said that we work the steps forward in recovery and we relapse through them backward. Once we have relapsed through the First Step and are using again, by definition we are no longer in recovery. The cup is full of crap again, we are looking at the gorgeous *outside* of the cup, and we have to start all over the process of emptying it out and creating useful space for connection to the world.

## Beginnings – Three

"The five colors
blind the eye.
The five notes
deafen the ear.
The five tastes
deaden the mouth."

*Tao Te Ching*, page 48

**Just Not There**
*Work, sleep, eat – Being.*
*Dream, laugh, wonder – non-Being.*
*Drink, snort, shoot up – un-Being.*

Some people in recovery have been fortunate enough to hear someone say to them, "Welcome to the human race. We've been waiting for you." I was. I now realize that my basic problem had not been stress or bad luck or foolish bosses or emotionally disturbed women or even the need to consume large amounts of alcohol and other drugs just to feel normal. My problem had been that I didn't want to belong to the human race. Too much pain accumulated from the deaths of Martin Luther King and Robert Kennedy and the Democratic Convention in Chicago when I was a phenomenally idealistic 17-year-old. Everything I believed in eroded almost at once, and after I chased the dream down the narrow-minded road of radical politics of the late 1960s and early 1970s, I said "fuck it" and fueled my journey to disconnection with alcohol and other drugs. Thirty-one years later, I ran out of gas. Along the way, I helped fuel the addictions of people I cared about.

Eventually, I got my wish about being separate from the human race. I was the person described in the Big Book on page 151:

"The less people tolerated us, the more we withdrew from society, from life itself. As we became subjects of King Alcohol, shivering denizens of his mad realm the chilling vapor that is loneliness settled down. It thickened, becoming blacker. Some of us sought out sordid places, hoping to find understanding companionship and approval. Momentarily we did – then would come oblivion and the awful awakening to face the hideous Four Horsemen – Terror, Bewilderment, Frustration, Despair."

Using addicts go straight from Being to un-Being every day. We can't experience non-Being because we feel too sorry for ourselves to just stop and *be alive*. Or as AA's co-founder, Bill Wilson, himself put it:

"No words can tell of the loneliness and despair I found in that bitter morass of self pity." (Big Book, p. 8).

Self pity is the enemy of spiritual growth, and 12-Step meetings are the enemy of self-pity because if you go to enough meetings in enough different places you will hear something that turns the thing causing you to feel sorry for yourself into the equivalent of, as they say, "leaves in the swimming pool."

We find relief only by being with people who had felt just like us and by practicing Step Eleven:

"Perhaps one of the greatest rewards of mediation and prayer is the sense of belonging that comes to us." (*Twelve Steps and Twelve Traditions*, p. 105).

When you truly belong, you don't think about it, you feel it.

**Beginnings – Four**

"Falling away at the frame of the bed.
Erosion.
Being steadfast: misfortune.

Falling away at the frame of the bed.
Lack of associates.

… the evil forces are growing gradually and steadily. … One at this place lacks wise teachers and helpful friends."

*The Complete I Ching*, pp. 208-209

**The Addict Who Went Back Out There**
for Mark M.

*His fall from grace*
*to hopelessness*
*began with leaves*
*flaming orange and red.*
*Winter iced up his despair.*
*But the leaves,*
*the leaves,*
*they never grew back.*

Grace is defined as a state of unmerited favor. In a state of grace, we have hope because we can't really identify any single behavior or action that has led to this grace. We don't know what we did to deserve it, just that we have it, and now that we have it, things look a lot better, and we don't want to lose it. When one appreciates grace, one appreciates the difference between justice and mercy. An important spiritual breakthrough happened to me in treatment (a rare occurrence for most) when I suddenly understood that for me it was not important why *some people died* when they *shouldn't* (unfair) but why some people *didn't die* when they *should* (grace). A week out of treatment someone in a meeting said, "It's a good thing life isn't fair. If it was, we'd all be dead."

The Mary Gauthier song *Mercy Now* says — "Every single one of us/Could use some mercy now/I know we don't deserve it/But we need it anyhow."

Once grace is lost, hopelessness replaces grace because the addict is now on his or her own, looking at the world with a diseased, ego-driven mind. The outside world looks like it does inside the addict's head. That's part of the egomania – if it seems this bad to the great and powerful Me, then it must this bad everywhere.

The best we can hope for in the battle with addiction is a scoreless tie every day. We can't win, no matter how long it is between drinks and other drugs. The Big Book and the accumulated experience of 12-Step recovery reports over and over that once an addict picks up the substance again, it rapidly gets worse than it was when he or she put the substance down. Not only do the amounts and frequencies rise above pre-quit levels, so do the consequences. The experience shared by those lucky enough to make it back from picking up again confirms this truth. If a spiritual life based simply on staying around our fellow sufferers at all costs will keep us from believing the Big Lie that it won't get worse, then whatever one calls "spirituality" is worth it for that alone.

> "The alcoholic at certain times has no mental defense against the first drink." (Big Book, p. 43)

The only defense is the other people in our program. They are the voice of our higher powers. If we disconnect from people, we die, first in our spirits, then in our minds, then in our bodies.

## Beginnings – Five

"What is going to be diminished
Must first be allowed to inflate.
Whatever you want to weaken
Must first be convinced of its strength.
You see, what is yielding and weak
Overcomes what is hard and strong."

*Tao Te Ching*, page 96

## The Levers of Addiction

*It uses our strengths,
not weaknesses.*

*Intellectual:
give up concepts.*

*Tough guy:
Cry like a baby.*

*Leader of men:
follow children.*

My primary strengths are and were intellect, rationality and a strong sense of justice. In my last several years of active addiction, I intellectualized, rationalized and justified everything, including nearly drinking myself to death. I thought my weaknesses were shyness (so I overcompensated with grandiosity) ... an inability to master one activity perfectly (there's a huge gulf between "lousy" and "perfect") ... and a sense that I was missing something that other people seemed to "get" instinctively (despite all appearances, the mass of men lead lives of quiet desperation). Again, I am way more interested in the concept of mercy than of justice and anyway, as Mose Allison put it — "Everybody's crying justice /Just as long as I get it first."

My strengths nearly killed me. My "weaknesses" are setting me free.

> "For just so long as we were convinced that we could live exclusively by our own individual strength and intelligence, for just that long was a working faith in a Higher Power impossible. It was only at the end of a long road, marked by successive defeats and humiliations, and the final crushing of our self-sufficiency, that we began to feel humility as something more than a condition of groveling despair. (*Twelve Steps and Twelve Traditions*, p. 72)

**Beginnings – Six**

"What is success and what is failure?

If you have prestige and favor,
all you worry about is that it will get taken away.
And if you have a lowly place, you are still basically afraid.
So both, at root, make for fear."

*Tao Te Ching*, page 51

**Fear**

*Vapor trails of my deeds*
*drift across the sky.*
*Someone will see them!*

*A tattered cloth wipes*
*my filthy face today.*
*Someone might take it!*

*Expectations of fools*
*await me tomorrow.*
*I might fail to meet them!*

Self-centered fear is the soul-poison that infects every active addict
and codependent.

"Driven by a hundred forms of fear, self-delusion, and self-pity, we
step on the toes of our fellows, and they retaliate. So our troubles,

11

we think, are basically of our own making. They arise out of ourselves, and the alcoholic is an extreme example of self-will run riot, though usually he doesn't think so." (Big Book, p. 62)

The Tao instructs that the only antidote to fear is love, the unconditional kind one gets from the other people in 12-Step programs. We may have anxiety about failing at our  job or not meeting someone's expectations of us or making the same mistakes over and over again or not knowing what to do next. But we need not *fear* any of these as long as we don't pick up again, as long as we keep asking for help, as long as we let the love of our fellow sufferers support us when we can't love ourselves and as long as we love them when they can't love *themselves*. People in recovery will say it was "Keep coming back" that meant so much to them early on. For me, it was "We'll love you until you learn to love yourself." I took full advantage of that because I knew some people around me didn't like me, but it looked like they *had* to love me. Later on, when my grandiosity and pompous proclamations began to fade away somewhat, some of them actually liked me, but by then I didn't *need* that because I had learned to love myself.  I need to be wanted in some fashion, but I don't often want to be needed anymore.

**Beginnings – Seven**

"Being steadfast and upright: good fortune.
Regret vanishes.
Nothing is unfavorable.
No beginning, there is an end.
Before changing, three days.
After changing, three days.
Good fortune."

*The Complete I Ching*, page 448


**Wanting It All Now**

*A horse runs too fast*
*for its carriage*
*& starts dragging*
*broken wheels.*
*Unable to run*
*any more,*
*never mind fast.*


Time is the addict's enemy and the recovering person's ally. Many addicts new to recovery want to fix all the damage they've caused in a few weeks or months, and thus skip over the unpleasant prospect of Steps Four-Eight and go right to Step Nine. The words "work" and "effort" appear in the Big Book at nearly every turn. 12-Step recovery is simple, but it is very hard. Only a strength driven first by belief and then by faith can help us persist in staying abstinent and working the Steps in the order they were written when a voice in our heads is always saying things like "You deserve a break" or

"Why are you spending so much time with all those boring people?" or "Why make amends to someone who screwed you over so badly?"

A frequent attendee at 12-Step meetings is the One-Nine-Twelve person, who says: "I'm an addict. I'm sorry. How can I help you?" We are told to slow down, keep it simple and let opportunities to make amends come to us. Our job, we are frequently told, is to *remain willing*, at all costs, to make amends and then clean house, trust "God" (whatever that is to the individual) and be of service.

> "...we consider how, with our newfound knowledge, we may develop the best possible relations with every human being we know. This is a very large order. It is a task which we may perform with increasing skill, but never really finish." (*Twelve Steps and Twelve Traditions*, p. 77)

**Beginnings – Eight**

"If you need to take action, only do what is necessary.
Never abuse your power.
And if you're successful, don't be smug."

*Tao Te Ching*, page 85

### Addict on a Roof

*A man builds*
*a mansion.*
*The roof is done.*
*He is full of pride,*
*standing on the peak.*
*But where is the ladder*
*he used to climb up?*
*No way to get down.*

"Remember that we deal with alcohol [and other drugs] – cunning, baffling, powerful!" (Big Book, pp. 58 & 59)

It has been said that "patient" should be added at the end of the above quote. Our disease will wait a long time to get us alone and kill us. It's only over if we die sober. Every relapse story begins with the same thing: "I quit going to meetings." These people forgot about the ladder that got them to the roof. They lost their humility. They didn't practice gratitude. They forgot what a powerful foe they were trying to keep at bay. They got bored. They lost their spiritual foundation, in other words.

**Beginnings – Nine**

"And that is why a huge army
With all its strength and complacency will be defeated:
Like a great tree axed down."

*Tao Te Ching*, page 181

### Strength

*The athlete*
*lifts up weights measured*
*in pounds.*
*The addict*
*sets down drugs measured*
*in ounces.*
*Way harder*
*to set down*
*than to lift.*

"Lack of power, that was our dilemma. We had to find a power
by which we could live, and it had to be a power greater than
ourselves. (Big Book, p. 45).

A huge army did not carve out the Grand Canyon. Water and wind
did. *Tao Te Ching* says that water is not only the most powerful force
on Earth, it is also the most humble because its nature is to seek the
lowest places. It takes extraordinary strength to *not* do something
that comes naturally to you – pick up a glass of whiskey and drink
it, roll up a joint and smoke it or find a new way to protect someone
from himself. This is what *wu wei* means — doing by not doing.

16

And no matter how much of this kind of anti-strength you have *gathered*, you can only *apply* it one day at a time.

Step One is simply saying, "My life, as I have run it, is broken." What can fix it? Step Two, for a start. Step Two is not about dominance or superiority or self-aggrandizement, the things we often associate with "getting ahead" and "staying strong." It's about coming to believe that something within you is naturally tuned into humility, patience and understanding, things many people associate with weakness.

> "With few exceptions our members find that they have tapped an unsuspected inner resource they presently identify with their own conception of a Power greater than themselves." (Big Book, p. 567-568)

At first, we were just too afraid, and then we were just too drunk or stoned, to know these things were in us. Oddly enough, many addicts are too egotistical in a kind of Alice in Wonderland way to forgive themselves and thus remove the greatest barrier to acceptance of their inherent humility, patience and understanding, which is shame.

> "In no deep or meaningful sense had we ever taken stock of ourselves, made amends to those we harmed, or freely given to any other human being without any demand for reward. ... Therefore we remained self-deceived, and so incapable of receiving enough grace to restore us to sanity." (*Twelve Steps and Twelve Traditions*, p. 32.)

> "Our human resources, as marshaled by the will, were not sufficient; they failed us utterly." (Big Book, p. 45)

The pathway to the inner strength, but not the strength itself, comes from outside, much like the Quakers say that Jesus is the best path to the Inner Light. In recovery, strength is in numbers; weakness is in isolation.

**Beginnings – Ten**

"Water over Fire.
An image of Already Fulfilled.
In correspondence with this,
The superior person contemplates the law of waxing and waning
And takes preventive measures against possible decline."

*The Complete I Ching,* page 487

### Recovery Path

*The path of the scholar
winds away from grace
and never returns
if he knows too much.
The path of the addict
winds away from grace
and comes back again
if he gives up knowing why.
What the scholar never found,
the addict never left.*

Albert Einstein once observed that in modern society we have a perfection of means and a confusion of ends. For many successful people in the world, a focus on results, not processes, is key to their success. For a recovering addict, this doesn't work. It's the other way around. It's the journey, not the destination.

If we get too far from the *process* of recovery and start focusing on the *results* of recovery, we run the risk of taking personal credit for what we've achieved. When we do this, humility has vanished and we listen to the demon's voice.

> "I found my tribe, the social architecture that fulfills my every need for camaraderie and conviviality. I learned how to live." (Big Book, p. 332)

Some people lose themselves in service work and don't go to many meetings. Or they become Big Book literalists who can't adapt a book written in 1939 to the 21st century and try instead to adapt the 21st century to 1939. Or they become monk-like recluses wrapped in a cloak of prayer and meditation who never share their experience, strength and hope with others. These people may be abstinent from alcohol and other drugs, but they aren't "sober" because spiritual and emotional sobriety requires that word dreaded by addicts everywhere – balance.

The movement from *yin* to *yang* and back again defines the change that accompanies the waxing and waning between opposites. It is the driving force of the Universe, according to Taoists. This change happens whether we're along for the ride or not. If we are out of balance and lost in one aspect of recovery, change will run us over, and we will be left there wondering what happened — until the next wave of change comes along and knocks us even further off balance.

This is a good place to address the granite-like resistance that most 12-Step members have to any changes in the way their meetings are conducted, where they take place, what time of day they take place, the order in which "How it Works" and "The Twelve Traditions" are read, what prayer is said at the end of the meeting and so on. This resistance, in my opinion, comes from the power of ritual, which was so powerful in their active addictions. It is adherence to ritual as a group, not resistance to change inside the individual, that would cause most 12-Step members to have an apoplectic fit if you suggested they read "The Twelve Traditions" first and then "How it Works" second. After all, the words are the same and what difference does it make whether one set of words is read before the other? It does, believe me.

## Beginnings – Eleven

"It is the Tao of spirit beings to harm the full
And bless the humble.
It is the Tao of humans to dislike the full
And love the humble.

Toiling humbly, the superior person.
The multitudes of people completely accept him."

*The Complete I Ching*, pages 151 & 152.


## Ego Deflation

*Dismantle a mountain*
*stone by stone.*
*Put it back together*
*stone by stone.*
*Same stones, but*
*the new mountain*
*looks different somehow.*

"These distinguished men had the nerve to say that most of the alcoholics under investigation were still childish, emotionally sensitive, and grandiose. How we alcoholics did resent that verdict! ... In the years since, however, most of us have come to agree with those doctors. ... We have seen that we were prodded by unreasonable fears or anxieties ... So false pride became the reverse side of that ruinous coin marked 'Fear.' (*Twelve Steps and Twelve Traditions*, p. 123)

"An egomaniac with an inferiority complex" is an exact description of me for most of my life. I suffered (and still do to some extent), from Superman or Bozo the Clown Syndrome. That is, I think I can do some particular difficult thing, and when it turns out that I can't, then I think I can't do *anything at all*. Priceless or worthless. Nothing in between. Many of us are like this.

Somehow, when I began to tear down the egomania, mostly through painful lessons of how to do recovery wrong, the feelings of inferiority subsided when I put myself back together. The accompanying grandiosity diminished (but never fully disappeared because this is a work in progress) because it did not have so much inferiority to make up for. To this day, I have no idea why that happened. I am grateful that it did, and I am also grateful I don't have an obsession to *know why* anymore.

**Beginnings – Twelve**

"If you go the Way of Tao, it can only be with you.
If you go the Way of Virtue, its purity will sustain you.

But if you go the way of loss, then that will be your name.
And if you cannot trust, no one will trust you."

*Tao Te Ching*, page 70

**Character Defects**

*Rocks piled on a slope*
*slide and tumble*
*not because of the nature*
*of the rocks*
*but because of the nature*
*of the slope.*

A famous *Pogo* comic strip says: "We have met the enemy, and he is us."

> "We learned that we had to fully concede to our innermost selves that were alcoholics. This is the first step in recovery." (Big Book, p. 30)

Once we do this, we have to get honest with the question, "Why did the seed of addiction fall on such fertile ground in me?" In my own case, a therapist once said I was "born with a broken heart" (hence my difficulty with the question, "When was I ever sane?")

I have a lot of Irish Catholics in my genetic makeup. My inherent ('endogenous" to use psychiatry-speak) depression and genetic predisposition to addiction are *explanations* of why I did what I did and what I was like, not *excuses* for what I did and what I was like. The one constant factor in all the bad decisions I made out of self-centered fear was me. I was the only one there for the whole show. I willingly applied an anti-depressant to one of my twin peaks of despair and the 12-Steps to the other one. To continue in recovery, I need to keep asking for help from my medical doctor and apply Steps Six and Seven to the rest of me, and I can't do that by myself because my way is the way of loss — loss of peace, loss of sanity, loss of life. *Tao* and *Te* will redeem me.

"After all, our problems were of our own making. Bottles were only a symbol. (Big Book, p. 103.)

**Beginnings – Thirteen**

"Water contained under Earth.
An image of Multitude.
In correspondence with this,
The superior person embraces people
And cares for the multitude."

*The Complete I Ching*, pages 89-90

### Walk On

*Which single thread in the rug
is the one that holds it together?
Which single person in recovery
is the one who keeps you clean?*

A sponsor in 12-Step programs is vital to working the Steps in order and with patience, dignity and grace. A sponsor, however, is someone you found in a 12-Step program, not at The Institute for Higher Human Functioning. To place all your faith and trust in one person, or even one small group of people, is foolhardy. To not have a sponsor (or trusted teacher) at all,  is even more foolhardy. Someone who sponsors himself has a fool for a sponsee. (See "The Teacher and His Student.")

Here is a place to talk about traits and defects. An introspective person who is driven by intuition and feeling will never be someone with 200 numbers of recovering people in his/her phone. Keeping to one's self by and large is a trait for that person. Completely isolating one's self from other people is that trait taken to an extreme and becomes what is called a "defect of character." Conversely, the extroverted person driven by activity and events and thinking goes to extremes when he/she is always busy with other people and never looks inward. The extrovert may appear to have a large group of recovery friends but only have superficial relationships with them, and the introvert may have a smaller group but one that can survive the meltdown of one of the group's members. Newcomers are often dismayed to see the number of people who melt down in 12-Step recovery. It is life-glue, not a panacea.

An old friend of mine said: "Coming into 12-Step programs and expecting to find fully healthy people is like going into the intensive care unit and expecting to find someone to play middle linebacker on your football team today."

> "It becomes plain that the group must survive or the individual will not." (*Twelve Steps and Twelve Traditions*, p. 130)

## Beginnings – Fourteen

"Usually people read because they want to know –
but the more you study the Tao, the less you want knowledge.

And as you want less and less, you come closer to not-doing.
*Wu wei* – this is the way things get done.

The best way to run the world
is to let it take its course
-- and to get yourself
out of the way of it."

*Tao Te Ching*, page 22

A pause for Rule 62.

## It's All About Me
## (Tao Joke I)

*To be in The Way*
*you have to*
*get out of*
*your own way.*

## Pass it Forward
## (Tao Joke II)

*Tao unto others*
*as you would have them*
*Tao unto you.*

**Beginnings -- Fifteen**

"The Tao goes on forever
*wu wei* – doing nothing.
And yet everything gets done."

*Tao Te Ching*, page 99

### The Wu-Wei Way

*Does craving fade
with good thoughts?
Or with no thoughts?
Craving starves
in the empty mind.*

"As we go through the day we pause, when agitated or doubtful, and ask for the right thought or action. ... We are then in much less danger of excitement, fear, anger, worry, self-pity or foolish decisions. We do not tire so easily, for we are not burning up energy foolishly as we did when we were trying to arrange life to suit ourselves. It works – it really does." (Big Book, pp. 87 & 88)

Many addicts have stacks of self-help books that they bought to help them figure out how to quit feeling so miserable. These books generally encouraged them to take their sick minds and compulsive behavior and use them to create a healthier way of thinking and acting. And these addicts would dutifully build up a "healthier" house of cards each day and promptly burn it down with alcohol and other drugs. A practicing addict cannot *help* himself. And a recovering addict cannot be helped *by himself.*

The self-help empire also encourages a lot of "positive feelings" and "finding your inner child." None of these help active addicts, who generally avoid any kind of feelings and who more than likely are terrified of their inner child, especially if they suffered abuse or neglect as a child. We know from a lot of research that addicts tend to have more native intelligence than the average person does, so what they do is think their way out of many problems.

But way too much thinking got many of us *into* recovery. Doing by not doing, turning off the thinking machine, leads us to virtue because virtue is inherent. It has been put another way: you can't think your way into right living, but you can live your way into right thinking. I recently heard a woman in recovery say, "When I first got sober, I didn't know what to do, so I did what I was told." No thinking, just acting. When confronted with this kind of proposal the highly intellectual addict will counter with "I can't do that all the time. I'm a doctor/airline pilot/business executive/professor/engineer/lawyer." No one is asking them to stop thinking all the time, just when it comes to the things that cause them to keep poisoning themselves and the lives of those around them despite their best thinking. I told an airline pilot once, "If we are first for takeoff, and you're in the captain's seat, and I'm in seat 32-B, I want you to be thinking *a lot* and in total control. When you're first in line at the grocery store, you need to let go of control. When you are walking by the airport bar after a flight, you need to quit thinking."

*Wu wei* is really just surrender, which is what 12-Step programs for addicts boils down to in one word. For codependents, the one word is detachment. Again, *wu wei* is the way. Doing nothing is absolutely the best way to help the addict in your life. Let him or her fall. Just don't be standing there at the *bottom* of the abyss when he or she falls over the *edge* of the abyss.

**Beginnings – Sixteen**

"Seeking union.
Those not having taken the first step:
Misfortune."

*The Complete I Ching*, page 97

### Love Among the Ruins

*Addicts love the idea*
*of oblivion*
*more than*
*oblivion itself.*
*This is why love*
*between two addicts*
*empties out quickly*
*if they try to love*
*way, way too soon.*

You will not find the admonishment, "No new relationships in the first year" in any of the conventional 12-Step literature. This advice to newcomers is, however, based on the painful experience of thousands of recovering people. What this advice or suggestion is talking about of course is a sexual relationship. Another way to put it is: you can have all the sex you want in the first year, and after that you can think about getting a partner. Especially dangerous for people in early recovery are intense relationships with other people in early recovery. The reason is those people have no idea who they really are, having blunted the reality of self by getting hammered all the time. And now he or she is going to share something that has just been born with another infant in the most intense and adult manner possible.

If you can have sex with someone with no emotional involvement whatsoever, then this doesn't apply to you. But if that's so, then you have a whole different set of problems. Only you can prevent narcissism.

Better to aim for two years with no new relationships. As with many other aspects of recovery, if we aim for perfection, we might get halfway there because our basic nature is to do enough to get by. We try to be like whatever we call God in order to get halfway there -- a decent human being.

David Foster Wallace, in his epic novel *Infinite Jest* (Little, Brown and Company, 1996), describes 13th Stepping -- the unsavory and incredibly unfair practice that some people have of hitting on newcomers – as an addition of the First and Twelfth Steps: my life is unmanageable; let me share it with you. He also got to the essence of the no new relationships suggestion in this novel:

> "This [not forming attachments to the opposite sex in a halfway house] is a corollary of Boston AA's suggestion that single newcomers not get romantically involved for the first year of sobriety. The big reason for this, Boston AAs with time will explain if pinned down is that the sudden removal of Substances leaves an enormous ragged hole in the psyche of the newcomer, the pain of which the newcomer's supposed to feel and be driven kneeward by and pray to have filled by Boston AA and the old Higher Power, and intense romantic involvements offer a delusive analgesic for the pain of the hole, and tend to make the involvees clamp onto one another like covalence-hungry isotopes, and substitute each other for meetings and Activity in a Group and Surrender, and then if the involvement doesn't pan out (which like how many between newcomers do you suppose do) both involves are devastated and in even more hole-pain than before and now don't have intensive-work-in-AA-dependent strength to make it through the devastation without

going back to the Substance. ... The no-involvement thing tends to be the Waterloo of all suggestions for newcomers, and celibacy's often the issue that separates those who Hang from those who Go Back Out There. (p. 1054)

**Beginnings – Seventeen**

"In the course of Chinese history, even now, almost every Chinese person knows and follows the truth of *pi ji tai lai*, meaning,

> Out of the depth of misfortune comes bliss.
> At the end of Hindrance comes Advance."

*The Complete I Ching*, page 127

**Prayer for Me**

*Thorns have roses.*
*No rain, no thorn.*
*Rain on me today.*

> "Those promises I thought were impossible are a viable force in my life. I am free to laugh all of my laughter, free to trust and be trusted, free to both give and receive help. I am free from shame and regret, free to learn and grow and work. I have left that lonely, frightening, painful express train through hell. I have accepted the gift of a safer, happier journey through life." (Big Book, p. 543)

The woman who wrote these words was once irritable, restless and discontent all at once, all the time. We all were.

How do we get out of addiction Hell? We set the bottle or the bag or the needle down and get up and walk out. The Demon says, "You can't do that!" And we say, "If you don't believe I'm leaving, just count the days I'm gone." And the Demon says,

"I'll come looking for you." And the Demon will, often when we are most unaware. But the true beginning is to realize that we are more miserable than we have ever been in our lives and that the misery can begin to stop as long as we stop using. From the bottom, we turn toward the top. But – no bottom, no top. No thorn, no rose.

And someday you might be able to say that you are not only grateful to be clean and sober, you are grateful to be an addict. I first heard someone say this during a "lead" talk at a treatment center, and I figured that they must pay that guy to go around to places like this and say that because it was the most preposterous thing I had ever heard. No one could actually mean that. But he did mean it, and I know why today. He had to go where he went and do what he did to get what he has, to quote a 12-Step meeting in the Portland area.

*Pi ji tai lai.*

BEGINNING

# WORK/EFFORT

"One who wishes to ascend needs an attitude of truthfulness and sincerity; otherwise, people will not lend support. [Growing Upward] uses the image of wood growing up from the earth. It takes effort for a tree's roots and trunk to break up the soil. ... One should cultivate virtue, build up character, accumulate knowledge and experience and work hard to establish credibility. This is the proper way to approach personal growth and promotion."

*The Complete I Ching*, page 370

"Chasing deer, no guide
In the midst of the woods.
The superior person is alert:
Give up!
Going forward: humiliation."

*The Complete I Ching*, page 58

### First Step

*Leaping tiger*
*rocks backward*
*before it leaps –*
*to gain power,*
*to preserve choice.*

"Our description of the alcoholic, the chapter to the agnostic, and our personal adventures before and after made clear three pertinent ideas:

(a) that we were alcoholic and could not manage our own lives
(b) that probably no human power could relieve our alcoholism.
(c) that God could and would if He were sought. (Big Book, p. 60)

Long-term use of alcohol and other drugs creates a lot of momentum. It's been said by some that simply stopping using is really Step Zero. Step One is the admission that our lives have been, up until this moment, out of control and full of misery, and the lack of control and misery are a function of our getting loaded all the time. So Step Zero involved, for most of us, the need to quit using even for a few hours and then step backward to get some perspective and some power. Then we can launch into an examination of the connection between powerlessness and unmanageability.

The ABCs of 12-Step recovery listed here (and read before every AA meeting I know of) show that one can't simply change direction when one is hell-bent for destruction. Border collies are masters at the full-speed change of course. Not so with addicts and the people around them. Children are taught to stop, drop and roll if their clothes catch on fire. Excellent advice for the addict whose *hair*, so to speak, is on fire.

The backward step also relates to the medical aspects of withdrawal from long-term use of drugs, especially ethanol and benzodiazepines. Alcohol/sedative addiction is a nasty disease in that it can kill you even when you're trying to run away from it. To suddenly quit drinking (and/or using benzos) heavily without medical supervision and anti-seizure medications is a very bad idea. Delerium tremens ("dancing with the snakes and bugs") are bad enough. The seizures that can accompany the DTs can kill you. Withdrawing from heroin ("kicking the bird") is extremely unpleasant. The withdrawing junkie may *wish* he or she could die, but the process of withdrawal itself won't do it. Not so with the chronic alcoholic/benzo user.

"Heaven and Earth
are not like humans.

They don't expect to be thanked
for making life,
so they view it without expectation."

*The Tao Te Ching*, page 35


## Second Step

*Your original face*
*has a sweet smile*
*for the you*
*who's coming back.*


This book began with this poem, a mere 13 words boiled down from many more. (See Foreword.) Tao is not judgmental. It doesn't care if someone strayed far from it or even if someone has come back to it. It doesn't care what we've done. It won't condemn us to eternal damnation for shooting dope or having sex with our neighbor's wife. It will, however, sustain us and never ask to be thanked for doing so. No sacrifices or offerings. No worship. *It just is* because that's all it needs to be—resonating truth and connection.

*(Note: The required active praying to one's Higher power for help is a problem for Taoists since you can't pray to Tao. I learned the term Tunkashila ("grandfather") from a Lakota Sioux in an NA step study meeting and use it as a form of address when I pray each morning for help in staying sober just one more day and send thanks*

*for another sober day, another miracle day, each night.)*

When I realized that the inherent purity of Tao has always been in me, I had true hope for the first time in my life. The need to measure Me against Them seemed less important. When I began to really practice the Second Step in this light, much of my fear about the future and not knowing what to do or say next disappeared. Recovery suddenly became more about not throwing away the chance to grow into something I had never imagined than it was about fear of going back to that cold, dark, lonely Hell (although I still have that fear, and newcomers and returning relapsers keep it alive for me).

> "We will comprehend the word serenity and know peace. No matter how far down the scale we have gone, we will see that our experience can benefit others. That feeling of uselessness and self-pity will disappear." (Big Book, p. 84)

Tao is like a wonderful dog that gives birth to itself and never dies.

"Follow the nothingness of the Tao,
and you can be like it, not needing anything,
seeing the wonder and the root of everything."

*Tao Te Ching*, page 27

## Third Step

*Decide to*
*step off the ledge*
*of your fear.*
*You have not done so much*
*that you will fall.*
*You have not done so little*
*that you will soar.*
*You will begin to be.*
*To do this once*
*is belief.*
*To do this twice*
*is faith.*

In one way or another, each of the Twelve Steps involves willingness, but the ones connected most explicitly to action (Four, Five, Seven, Nine, Ten and Twelve) all require willingness first and foremost.

> "We find that no one need have difficulty with the spirituality of the program. *Willingness, honesty and open mindedness are the essentials of recovery. But these are indispensable.*" (Big Book, p. 568)

When I first encountered this step, I was fiercely resistant. Then a treatment professional, whose job it was to wake me up, hit me upside the head with a figurative two-by-four and said, "You don't want any of this. You're just here looking for more *data*." She said "data" in a manner much like that of a cat coughing up a hairball. I had been sober for 11 days at that point, and in the few minutes following that figurative head-bashing, I had an overpowering urge to get as drunk as I could. My M.O. was: "You hurt me, so I'm going to hurt me, too."

But since I was in a treatment center far from any liquor store, to act on that urge would have required a strenuous effort, and the urge passed. In the next few weeks, I learned that my fear of saying, "I don't know" is what kept me from believing in the Third Step, so I looked that fear in the eye and made a decision to turn my will and my life over to the care of this vague Higher Power thing that I didn't believe in but was told that didn't matter.

I could not have done this without being utterly beaten down by the disease, my counselors and a few of the other men on my unit in the treatment center. I was in 12-Step kindergarten. After 28 days, I went straight from recovery kindergarten to recovery middle school and life among hard-core AAs and NAs who said the same things I heard in the treatment center, but many of these people *wanted* to be there. In fact, some of them seemed pretty damn *happy* about it.

> "If you have decided you want what we have and are willing to go to any length to get it – then you are ready to take certain steps." (Big Book, p. 58)

This quote from the Big Book defines Step Zero, as noted above. I now realize I have to make the decision to step off the ledge of my fear every day. I don't fear the Third Step because I now have *faith* that it works. It's been said that Columbus believed (or he really, really *hoped*) that the world was round when he first set sail for the New World. After that, he had faith that it was round because he didn't sail off the edge of the earth the first time. This is much like the accomplished ski jumper. He had to go down that ramp the first time absolutely dripping with fear. But more experienced ski jumpers told him to keep his ski tips up and bend his knees on landing.

Most of us have *seen* and *felt* the power of the Third Step in our lives and in those of hundreds of other people. Addicts are not going to spend the rest of their lives chasing a vague promise of something better. We have to see it. We have to be hit over the head with it. It has to be so clear that even our addled, rationalizing minds cannot deny it. But even with all that, we have to be *willing* to see it.

> "Practicing Step Three is like the opening of a door which to all appearances is still closed and locked. All we need is a key, and the decision to swing the door open. There is only one key, and it is called willingness." (*Twelve Steps and Twelve Traditions*, p. 34)

The predecessor step to this one is Step Two. A lot of people new to 12-Step recovery get hung up on that step because they think it asks them to already have a conception of a Higher Power and some spiritual practice with which to reach it. It doesn't say that. It says we came to believe it's *possible* that a higher power *could* restore us to sanity. Not that it will, but that it could, a conditional word based on the next nine steps that produce a promise in Step 12 — "having had a spiritual awakening as a result of these steps …" So if one has obtained a belief in a possibility, one is more willing to take the next of the following nine steps.

"Watching one's own life.
To advance or to retreat?
One should not lose one's way."

*The Complete I Ching*, page 188


## Fourth Step

*If our lives
are gardens
in need of weeding,
we first must know
which roots make weed
and which make garden.*


Twelve-Step recovery is full of Three-Step Waltzers, who go "one, two, three ... out!" in 3/4 waltz time over and over again. These people have a profound fear of the Fourth Step for any number of reasons. Generally, the block is not having worked Step Three completely (still have fear of looking inward) or fear of Step Five (have a fear of exposing one's inner self). But:

> "This perverse soul-sickness is not pleasant to look upon. Instincts on rampage balk at investigation. The minute we make a serious attempt to probe them, we are liable to suffer severe reactions." (*Twelve Steps and Twelve Traditions*, p. 44)

The fear many of us feel when looking at this step comes from the fact that the *last things* we want to look at are resentment, fear and guilt. We drink/use/gamble/eat/control to make those things *go away*. But when we overcome this fear and keep it simple,

45

many of us find that what we thought was good about ourselves was, in fact, bad, and what we thought was bad about ourselves was, in fact, good. We need a lot of help and guidance and patience with this step because when we first get into recovery, we have no idea what is weed and what is garden. We don't even know where the garden *is* most of the time.

> "Therefore, we started upon a personal inventory. This was Step Four. A business which takes no regular inventory usually goes broke. Taking a commercial inventory is a fact-finding and a fact-facing process. It is an effort to discover the truth about the stock-in-trade. One object is to disclose damaged or unsalable goods, to get rid of them promptly and without regret. If the owner of the business is to be successful, he cannot fool himself about values. (Big Book, p. 64)

"No one likes the honest truth,
and all fine talk falls short if it.

Real words are never used to seduce you,
and those that do are no good."

*Tao Te Ching*, page 191


**Fifth Step**
*Say it to:*
*yourself – addiction listens*
*yourself and God – yearning listens*
*yourself and God and another human being –*
*Tao listens.*


My own words only seduce me to return to the state of mind in which I believe that it's OK for me to drink alcohol, drop acid or smoke marijuana. I can't speak to the Tao, even though it listens to everything. I can only know that there are times when something I'm thinking, feeling or doing is *not*-Tao. A Christian can admit his or her faults to Jesus, but he or she cannot *hear* Jesus giving feedback. An analog of Jesus — a priest for instance, is needed. Buddhists have an advantage in that they know a professed direct link to Buddha is a sign not of holiness, but of derangement.

" ... what comes to us alone may be garbled by our own rationalization and wishful thinking ... It is worth noting that people of very high spiritual development almost always insist on checking with friends and spiritual advisers the guidance they feel they have received from God." (*Twelve Steps and Twelve Traditions*, p. 60)

The other human being involved in this step is the agent of maximizing the balance between *yin* and *yang* in the recovering addict's life or creating the potential for such balance later on.

Taking this step for the first time is, to many recovering addicts, an incredibly liberating moment. It is experiencing freedom from our own insanity. It is also practice of the utmost importance. We open up with another person, tell him or her things we probably never told anyone before and find in the future that it is now much easier to open up to other people, to share our feelings openly and honestly, to own up to our mistakes, to look straight ahead instead of over our shoulders or down at the ground all the time (see Step Ten).

> "Provided you hold back nothing, your sense of relief will mount from minute to minute. ... As the pain subsides, a healing tranquility takes its place." (*Twelve Steps and Twelve Traditions*, p. 60)

"Remedying.
Sublimely prosperous and smooth.
Favorable to cross great rivers.
Before starting, three days.
After starting, three days.

It indicates that every ending follows a new beginning.
This is the course of Heaven."

*The Complete I Ching*, page 172


### Sixth Step

*That snow was cold.*
*I stayed inside.*
*That stream was deep.*
*I stayed on the bank.*
*That sand was hot.*
*I stayed in the shade.*
*That road was rough.*
*I stayed home.*

*We find ourselves*
*unwilling to move on.*
*Afraid  to cross*
*from then into when,*
*where we can love again.*


Step Six is the Step One for relief of everything beyond relief of
the manic and unstoppable ingestion of alcohol and other drugs,
the need to place one more bet, the desire to binge on a gallon of

ice cream and purge it, the need to interfere pointlessly in another person's life one more time. Time and the process of working the first five steps get most addicts beyond the infernal craving of their first few weeks and months. Then, to quote the author Earnie Larsen, they run into the mountain, and the mountain is them.

> "Having been granted a perfect release from alcoholism, why then shouldn't we be able to achieve by the same means a perfect release from every other difficulty or defect? This is a riddle of our existence, the full answer to which may be only in the mind of God." (Twelve Steps and Twelve Traditions, p. 64)

The answer to this question is in a Grateful Dead song: "When push comes to shove, you're afraid of love."

There are many ways to cope with fear, but the only antidote to fear is love. The fear knows this.

"Decreasing and being sincere and truthful
There will be supreme good fortune.
Without fault.
One can be steadfast and upright.
It is favorable to have somewhere to go."

*The Complete I Ching*, page 335

### Seventh Step

*Envy, guilt, rage,*
*blame and shame.*

*Five cards in your hand.*
*Fold them all.*
*Why discard envy,*
*guilt and rage and*
*draw to blame and shame?*

"We will want to be rid of some of these defects, but in some instances this will appear to be an impossible job from which we recoil. And we cling with a passionate persistence to others which are just as disturbing to our equilibrium, because we still enjoy them too much. How can we possibly summon the resolution and the willingness to get rid of such overwhelming compulsions and desires?" (*Twelve Steps and Twelve Traditions*, p. 673)

The chapter on Step Seven in *Twelve Steps and Twelve Traditions* answers its own question. The answer is humility. At first, most addicts achieve humility only through humiliation. But it doesn't have to be that painful. The root sense of the word "humility" is "humble." This is what Alfred Huang, in *The Complete I Ching* (p. 153) has to say on the 15th symbol -- Humbleness.

> "One can see how much value was placed on the quality of humility by the ancients. To them, humbling oneself did not mean to act negatively by holding oneself back. Instead one should act positively by doing something with other people cooperatively and harmoniously. The key is to respect people and treat them equally. Only in this way can true peace and harmony be established in the community."

This paragraph is what led me to wonder if some ancient Chinese sage with some leftover soul-sickness to clean up didn't come back to life as William Griffith Wilson in Vermont in 1895.

"Heaven with Fire.
An image of Seeking Harmony.
In correspondence with this,
The superior person makes classifications of people
According to their natures
And makes distinctions of things
In terms of their categories."

*The Complete I Ching*, page 136


**Eighth Step**

*Our lists evolve
like seasons with names
that fall off branches
and grow back again
or that fall to
make the compost
of our forgiveness.*


An astute observation is: "Addicts are just like other people, only more so." Early in their lives, many addicts and codependents are acutely, or *perversely*, aware of distinctions between people according to which group at school they are "in" with or what their boyfriends/girlfriends look like or how they dress. Later, as big-time abusers of chemicals or people, they classify people according to how much power they have or how accomplished their children are or the pithy things they say at parties and so on. To classify people according to their inherent natures is foreign to us, and that's another reason we slip into isolation from humanity, even when we are in the midst of hundreds or thousands of human beings.

Having done the Fourth Step, people in recovery have a handy list of people they have harmed. A tremendous breakthrough in my own recovery was discovering that much of the harm I did to other people was not so much in what I did *to them* (sins of commission) but in what I could have done *for them* but didn't (sins of omission).

I was talking to my first AA sponsor about how I had cut all these people out of my life, and he said, "What about all the people who wanted into your life, and you didn't even know it?"

The Alanon 12-Step program encourages its members to always include themselves on their Eighth Step lists. Out of forgiveness of self comes love of self. (See next entry.)

> ".. it is equally necessary that we extricate from an examination of our personal relations every bit of information about ourselves and our fundamental difficulties that we can. Since defective relations with other human beings have nearly always been the immediate cause of our woes, no field of investigation could yield more satisfying and valuable personal rewards than this one." (*Twelve Steps and Twelve Traditions*, p. 80)

"Seeking harmony.
Begins with crying and weeping.
Ends with laughing.
The great multitude succeeds in meeting."

*The Complete I Ching*, page 137

### Ninth Step

*A man can make amends*
*to the forest he cut down*
*by planting new trees.*
*A man can make amends*
*to the love he destroyed*
*only by loving himself*
*again ...*
*for once ...*
*at all.*

It is significant that the so-called Promises in the Big Book (pp. 83 & 84) are said to come true during the process of working the Ninth Step. Jumping ahead to this step is misguided and often destructive because the recovering addict takes a long time to love himself or herself again, if he or she ever did. When we do this step, we are essentially asking someone to forgive us, and if we can't forgive ourselves, why should we expect other people to do it (see page 17)? In Steps Five, Six and Seven, we forgive ourselves for our character defects and then become willing to have them removed. In Step Eight, we can write down our own name on the list of people we have harmed. When we do that, we are capable of self-love.

When I began to work this step with constant guidance from my sponsor, I realized what I was doing was taking ownership for behavior that wasn't really "my fault" because I was sick from addiction and depressed as hell to boot. And claiming as my own what wasn't really "my fault" is what made it so easy for me to be forgiven.

Further, taking responsibility for something that wasn't really my fault made it far easier for me to get humble and honest and take immediate responsibility for things that *are* my fault. Conveniently, the step in which I own up to things that are my fault immediately follows the one in which I take responsibility for things that aren't. (See Step Ten)

The Promises fall where they do in the process because everything before that is about generating the *willingness* to do something incredibly foreign to us. That is why we begin to intuitively know how to handle things that used to baffle us. We got willing to look at things a different way. We were baffled because we were blind.

Three days before my last drink/drug, I denied an accusation of being drunk at work but nonetheless confessed to my boss that I was incredibly messed up, and she said, "It's good to hear you say that because you have a meeting with the Employee Assistance Program in 20 minutes." Busted!

The EAP sent me to treatment, treatment sent me to a 12-Step program, the program sent me to AA and AA sent me to the Tao. I have done a Ninth Step with this same former boss. I was terrified when I saw her sitting there at a restaurant table, and all my old resentments and fears of her welled up in me. But I went ahead on because I was committed to it. By then I had some integrity that I couldn't seem to ignore. I had remained willing to do this, and now here was the time. We got around to that moment when she told me I had a meeting with the EAP in 20 minutes, and I told her that somewhere *during* those 20 minutes my life changed. And she said what happened to me *after* those 20 minutes was one of the most significant things that ever happened in *her* life. We sat there in that restaurant and cried. Together.

> "Our whole attitude and outlook upon life will change." (Big Book, p. 84)

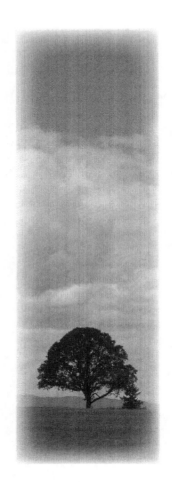

"If the true Tao is lost
then morality takes its place.

If that fails, we have 'conscience.'
When that fades, we get 'justice.'

When that disappears, we have the status quo."

*Tao Te Ching*, page 102

### Tenth Step

*A clumsy stroke*
*results in a smudge.*
*A wrong turn*
*results in no arrival.*
*A wrong done*
*unadmitted*
*results in going backward.*

Imagine a man who sets out to rob a bank, stops at a convenience store to get some liquid fortitude for the bank job and then realizes that the guy in line in front of him has a knife in his hand and is robbing the store. Because he is irritated at this delay in his acquisition of liquid fortitude, he stabs the robber with his *own* knife and subsequently is given a big reward and lots of praise for saving the lives of the convenience store clerk and the other customers because it turns out the robber had killed people in other convenience-store robberies.

Is this man a hero? Not in a 12-Step program he isn't, because *how it worked out* is not the point. *What you meant to do is.*

When we get to Step Ten, we are beginning to live in the solution. Everything before that is about identifying the problem or plowing the ground. The potential bank robber is not a hero because if he is *fully honest* with himself and what he is doing, he has to admit that he meant to steal someone's money, not save someone's life. A recovering addict who lies to someone and figures it's not a problem because that person never found out about the lie is going backward in his or her program. Quickly.

It is inherently wrong, or not-Tao, to drive a 4,000-pound deadly weapon down the street when you are intoxicated. The law also says it's wrong, but if you drive drunk or stoned and don't get caught, you may not be in trouble with the law, but you still did something wrong. Someone who drives drunk or stoned hundreds of times with no DUI arrests is *just as guilty* of the crime as the person who does felony-type time for it. *How it worked out* is not the point.

When an entire society loses its conscience, it relies on justice. We in recovery, though, must be driven by something that supercedes justice. It's called "doing the next right thing." It is called valuing mercy, as in Mary Gauthier's song (see page 8). This is also called virtue, which connects us to true Tao.

*What I meant to do* runs head on into the old saying that the road to Hell is paved with good intentions. This is especially problematic for the codependent, who has said over and over, "I'm just trying to help him/her," while he/she is yelling, "Stop with the helping!" But helping someone when they didn't ask for help or when they ought to be able to do something for themselves is do-goodism. It's the same ego out of control that the drunk or junkie has. It's like letting someone know you love them by thinking about them.

This dynamic changes when we are able to say to someone, "It didn't seem to bother you, but I really wanted to hurt you when I said that particular thing. That was really wrong of me." When we are able to perform this kind of check on ourselves, we find that our behavior falls more in line with our values, and that may be the best gift of all in recovery.

A recovering alcoholic who is a Catholic nun told me once that what she does as a nun is one thing. That's her religion. What she did in 12-Step recovery was something else. That's spirituality. She said that the spiritual sickness of addiction is caused by our behavior being so out of line with our own values. Only a sociopath has no value system. So, she said, someone who can say, "What I do is what I believe" is a spiritual person. Not so cosmic, is it?

No one, especially those with some time in recovery, will give any credence to our intentions if our behavior is constantly out of line with them, anyway. It's been put this way: your priorities are what you're doing. If you've been in recovery awhile and you are not sneaking drinks or drugs and are visibly and openly cleaning house, trusting your higher power and being of service to other people in recovery, then what you *intend* to do is right in line with what you actually *are* doing. Bars around the world are full of people who talk about what they intend to do "some day." But they never do it. The person who tells his sponsor, "I was going to call you, but then I had to take care of something else" is not living in the solution. The one who says, "I was going to call you, but I was just too afraid to do it" is.

> "Our next function is to grow in understanding and effectiveness. This is not an overnight matter. It should continue for our lifetime. Continue to watch for selfishness, dishonesty, resentment, and fear. When these crop up, we ask God at once to remove them. We discuss them with someone immediately and make amends quickly if we have harmed

anyone. Then we resolutely turn our thoughts to someone we can help. Love and tolerance of others is our code. (Big Book, p. 84)

A spiritual corollary of Step Ten is its philosophical opposite – continued to take personal inventory, and when we did something good for another person took no credit for it. When you are living in the solution, you have gone from "It's all about me" to "It has nothing to do with me." The active addict thinks, "What can I get away with today?" The recovering addict thinks, "What can I do to help someone else today?" The beauty of 12-Step recovery is that the purpose of thinking how to help someone else is not purely philanthropic or done so people will like you better or to earn God points but rather to help yourself. When all else fails, help another addict. That's how you help yourself. A perfect path for the self-centered, hedonistic person we were and frequently still are.

"Heaven and earth are like a pair of bellows;
they are empty, and yet they can never be exhausted.

Work them, and they produce more and more –
there's too much talking; it's really better to stay quiet."

*Tao Te Ching*, page 35

### Eleventh Step

*Help me.*
*Show me.*
*Lead me.*
*Undo me.*

One of the more valuable suggestions handed down in 12-Step programs is this: work the program that's in the Book, not the one people talk about in meetings.

So:

> "We may not be able to determine which course to take. Here we ask for inspiration, an intuitive thought or a decision. We relax and take it easy. We don't struggle. We are often surprised how the right answers come after we have tried this for awhile. What used to be the hunch or the occasional inspiration gradually becomes a working part of the mind. Being still inexperienced and having just made conscious contact with God, it is not probable that we are going to be inspired at all times. We might pay for this presumption in all sorts of absurd actions and ideas. Nevertheless, we find that our thinking will,

as time passes, be more and more on the plane of inspiration. We come to rely upon it." (Big Book, p. 87)

The program that's in the book says that we need to have a higher power in our lives, one that talks and acts through other people in recovery in most cases. We need to ask this power for help staying sober every day every morning and thank it if that happens every night. We need it, again in the form of other people, to show us where to go and where not to go (this is what "stick with the winners" means). We need it to lead us out of the despair and fear and hopelessness that are the features of our addictive operating systems. And we need it to undo the experience of un-Being so that we can live in the wonder of non-Being.

Clean house, trust "God" and be of service are the three legs of the recovery stool. Step Ten is cleaning house (constantly), and Step Eleven is trusting "God" (goodness and rightness). Step Twelve is being of service. If we can manage to live in these three steps, we will not only stay clean and sober, we will have something valuable to give away. And the true beauty of 12-Step recovery, as noted above, is that when all else fails, we can only help ourselves by giving what we have to someone else. The "wealthiest" person in the history of 12-Step recovery is the one who has given the most away.

"I trust those who trust me.
I also trust those who have no faith in me:
What I give, I receive."

*Tao Te Ching*, page 125

## Twelfth Step (10⁸ x 6)

*If ten people each*
*helped ten other people*
*each of whom*
*helped ten other people*
*each of whom*
*helped ten other people*
*each of whom*
*helped ten other people*
*each of whom*
*helped ten other people*
*each of whom*
*helped ten other people*
*each of whom*
*helped ten other people*
*each of whom*
*helped ten other people*
*each of whom*
*helped only six other people*
*everyone on earth*
*would be helped*
*if only just once.*

*Can you find*
*ten addicts to help?*

Step Twelve contains a promise – it says that if you have willingly, honestly and with an open mind worked the first Eleven Steps, you will experience a spiritual awakening. This is actually where Step Two comes to fulfillment. It doesn't say, "Having worked these steps, there's a pretty good chance you will have had a spiritual awakening by now." In the same vein, the Fifth Chapter of the Big Book is called "How It Works," not "How It Comes Out OK Sometimes When You Get Around to Feeling Like Doing It." So we are promised the gift of a spiritual awakening, one that will not only keep us out of addiction or codependency Hell but make our lives far simpler, less baffling and more rewarding than they were, for some people inconceivably so.

Two obligations come with the gift. The first is to help other addicts who are still suffering, and this doesn't mean just those who are still Out There. It means the old timer who lost a child. It means the person with six months who is dreading the Fourth Step. It means the person with seven or eight years clean and sober who is drifting away from the program.

The poem in this section is an 82-word recipe for eliminating all the armies, police forces and social welfare agencies in the world. Utopia? Certainly, but it does show that something given to ten other people from one person can, through the amazing power of geometric progression, spread far. AA started as three people in 1935. In the early 21st century, 70-some years later, it comprises more than three million people. That's a growth of $3 \times 10^6$. The number's far higher when you factor in NA, OA, Alanon and all the other 12-Step programs. $6 \times 10^8$ helps every person on earth. That doesn't seem so far from $3 \times 10^6$.

This Utopian process cannot begin, however, if someone waits for the other guy to do it. Imagine a 12-Step meeting with 20 people sitting in a circle. Each person in the circle looks at the person to his or her immediate right and thinks, "I'll let him/her come to the meeting tomorrow. I don't feel like it." The next day, a person who has been clean and sober for a few hours comes to that meeting, miserable as hell and looking to finally surrender. Who is there to carry the message to that new person? None of the 20 people from the day before, that's for sure.

The second obligation is to practice the principles we learned in the first Eleven Steps in all our affairs. Again, a 12-Step program is much like practice in the golf game of life. You get to practice on other members how to be open with your feelings, appreciative of little favors done you, honest in your financial dealings and humble in your general approach to the world.

> "Then he asked for the grace to bring love, forgiveness, harmony, truth, faith, hope, light and joy to every human being he could." (*Twelve Steps and Twelve Traditions*, p. 101).

We practice on other drunks and addicts and codependents and overeaters and sex addicts and compulsive gamblers so that our game is more finely tuned when we're out there in The World, where everyone's keeping score and mistakes can be fatal.

The point of all 12-Steps programs is to return us to The World as more functional and contributing people than we were before. Many of people out there ("normies" or "earthlings") find that certain people in recovery are among the most reliable, caring, insightful and dedicated people they have ever met. The reason for this was put well by Ernest Hemingway: "Life breaks everyone. Some people grow back stronger at the broken places."

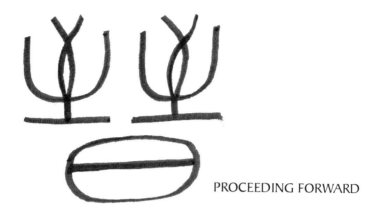

PROCEEDING FORWARD

# FELLOWSHIP

"In the time of diversity, one should be generous and magnanimous. In dealing with bad people, it is not necessary to keep a good distance from them. Even encountering them face to face, there would be no fault. ... to smooth out a misunderstanding takes time; the lost horse will come back of its own accord. With the proper attitude, even in meeting a person with different ideas there will be no problem."

*The Complete I Ching*, page 317

"Being sincere and truthful,
Not to the end.
Confused,
Still bringing together.
If crying out,
Once grasping hands: laughing.

Do not worry,
Going forward: no fault."

The Complete I Ching, page 362


**Unity**
*Notes in sequence
make a melody.*

*Notes in unison
make a chord.*

*The active addict sings
a warped melody
no one else hears.*

*The recovering addict
dances to the rhythm
of a celestial chord.*

If we put ourselves ahead of our group, we will lose ourselves because we will start drinking/using/betting/obsessing again. If we put one person or a small group of people ahead of the group, we will lose ourselves *and* them for the same reason. Anything we put ahead of recovery, we are going to lose anyway. Perhaps a man meets a woman who never knew him when he was drinking. He picks up again, and where does she go? Down the highway, Jim. All of this relates to the fact that addiction is progressive. Alcoholics Anonymous members will say to the alcoholic still Out There, "So you hate your job? OK. Just keep on drinking, and you won't have it to hate anymore."

Benjamin Franklin addressed the point perfectly a long time ago: "We must hang together or surely we will hang separately."

Remember, too, that most of The World doesn't give a damn that we got clean or sober. No head of state is going to give us a medal for acting like normal, responsible people for a change. I heard someone say once, "A recovering alcoholic is the only person in the world who expects to get an award for accepting a gift." The only people who can really appreciate what we've gone through, or are about to go through, are other people in recovery. If we look beyond them for affirmation, we had better also look beyond them for a headstone. A perfect epitaph for that person: "Well, he won't keep coming back."

> "Realization dawns that he is but a small part of a great whole; that no personal sacrifice is too great for preservation of the Fellowship." (*Twelve Steps and Twelve Traditions*, p. 130)

"To see yourself as extraordinary
is to stand out like jade among ordinary stones;
but what people ignore – the lonely and the worthless
is the rock a true leader finds himself on.

You see, you win by losing – and you lose by succeeding."

*Tao Te Ching*, page 105


## One, Many

*No one's in charge,*
*except for those who are.*
*No one speaks for others*
*except when they speak for themselves.*
*No one understands*
*except that they don't understand.*
*No one is in the group*
*unless the group is in them.*
*I lead them*
*so that they can lead me.*
*We sit in a group*
*so we can walk alone.*


Many people outside 12-Step recovery get incredibly frustrated trying to understand it because it is so full of paradox, so counter-intuitive, so unlikely on the face of it to work like any other social institution. But Twelve-Step recovery is unlike any other social institution because the people in it are unlike non-addicted people in many ways, yet they are exactly like *one another* in *one* way. In a sense, these groups are perfect manifestations of theoretical Marxist economics. The "excess value of labor" in a 12-Step "economy" not only returns to the individual, it returns in far greater magnitude than what the individual put in. "Pay it forward" is the only way to pay it back.

Twelve-Step recovery is Tao. If you can describe why it works, you probably don't know what it is, as the next section makes clearer. The chapter beginning on page 58 of the Big Book is "How it Works," not "Why it Works."

"If you know what it is, don't talk it away.
If you do, then you don't understand."

*Tao Te Ching*, page 138

## Third Tradition

*A want is not
a need.
A need is not
a desire.
A desire is all
you need
if you want it.*

Ninety percent of the people who need 12-Step recovery never find it. A lot of the people who do need it and discover after awhile that they *want* it, end up throwing it away because they forget that they need it. A sincere desire to repeat the process daily, to reinvent ourselves as recovering people is all we need, and the only requirement for membership in 12-Step programs for addicts is a desire to stop using.

If you are early in recovery, and if you have not used or drank or gambled or binged on food or controlled someone today, and if you have been to or will be at a meeting within 24 hours of now, and if you wish to complain bitterly about not getting something you want, you might want to follow this blunt suggestion given to me when I was about three months sober. I called a old-timer to complain about something, and he said, "Shut up. You have everything you need. All the rest of this is about what you want." I realize "shut up" is too harsh for many people, but it has kept me on the right path more than once. This is much like a little scene written by Ring Lardner in which a young boy (Lardner) asks his father why they left a place so early. "Shut up," he explained.

> "... we do become grateful for the necessity to toe the line ..." (Big Book, p. 275)

"Things have been given names from the beginning.
We need to know when we have enough names: this is wisdom."

*Tao Te Ching*, page 89

## Anonymity

*With no names,*
*no labels.*
*With no labels,*
*no ranking.*
*With no ranking,*
*no status.*
*With no status,*
*no power.*

*I have no power.*

*You have no power.*

*Together we are*
*powerful.*

In the United States, the first question someone generally asks when introduced to a stranger is, "What do you do?" They mean, "What is your job?" In 12-Step programs, you can know someone for months or years and have no idea what their job is. But even if you do know it, that piece of information is irrelevant. Many of us have been in a meeting with both wealthy people and street people. One person may have come to the meeting in a Cadillac, and a street person may have walked a long way. But for the purposes of the meeting, once it starts, those two people are exactly the same. The person in the Cadillac may have been clean/sober for 10 years, and the street person may have been clean/sober for 10 days but, again, for the purposes of that meeting at that time on that day, they are exactly the same. The old saw is, "Whoever got up earliest today has been sober the longest."

Anonymous literally means "having no name." The first three members of Alcoholics Anonymous were a stockbroker, a surgeon and a lawyer. (I sometimes wistfully wish that Bill Wilson had been a Native American so that they would have been a doctor, lawyer and an Indian chief, presaging a popular song by 10 years and Bo Diddley by even more years.)

It is a natural human instinct to rank people by their social status, but it is unnatural in 12-Step programs when they work well. Stockbroker Bill Wilson and Dr. Bob Smith did not introduce themselves to AA number three as such. The first two brought in the third because they said, "My name is Bill, and I'm an alcoholic." and, "My name is Bob. Here's how I used to drink." The lawyer heard his own story.

ABOLISHING THE OLD

# THE STUDENT
# AND HIS TEACHER

" So, a good man is a model for a bad one.
And, misguided, he is touched by his goodness.

Not to follow a teacher here
Or to love his precious message
Is to lose the Way, however clever you are –
This is the essence of the matter."

*Tao Te Ching*, page 78

(The teacher's comments in this section are in italics.)

## Pick up the Phone

The student said to his teacher:
"I needed your help and called,
but you weren't home."

*That is how I helped you.*


## In Sobriety

The student said to his teacher:
"I am told I am living the life
I could have had without addiction."

*Then you should give thanks
for your addiction.*


## Making a Decision

The student asked his teacher:
"If I give my will and life
to the care of God,
what will I have left for me?"

*Everything that you
never noticed before.*

## Plowing the Field

The student asked his teacher:
"How do I know
what God's will is for me?"

*What are you doing today mostly?*

"I am recovering from addiction."

*Do you find this difficult?*

Very.

*Then why would God
want more from you?*

## Who Am I?

The student asked his teacher:
"Who am I if I suppress the addict?"

*No one. That is how
I became everyone.*

# Pendulum

The student asked his teacher:
"How do you come back
to center so quickly?"

*My pendulum*
*has little weight.*
*The wind blows me,*
*and I twirl.*
*A man pushes me;*
*I do not swing.*
*I cannot move*
*far from center*
*because I am so light.*

"How can I achieve lightness?"

*Comparison makes*
*your pendulum heavy.*
*This and that.*
*This or that.*
*If not this,*
*then that.*
*Hard to move you.*
*Hard to stop you.*
*Do not compare;*
*you will return to center.*

"And this will make me better?"

*You are comparing again.*

**Confusion**

The student asked his teacher:
"Why am I confused?
Am I missing something?"

*The recovering person
embraces confusion.
It means you think
like a newly hatched bird*

**Fairness**

The student said to his teacher:
"My friend is recovering,
but his children died.
This seems so unfair."

*The fair comes to town
once a summer.*

## Naked (Truly)

A student of many years
was told to remove his clothes.
He did this entirely, but still
his teacher was not satisfied.

"But I am standing here stark naked!"

*You haven't taken off your mask.*

"Damn it! What mask?"

*The one that covers
your original face.*


## Passing it Forward

The student asked his teacher,
who was very old:
"What do I do
when you are gone?"

*I hope you
and your students
dance on my grave.*

# Bibliography

Anonymous, *Alcoholics Anonymous*, Alcoholics Anonymous World Services, New York 2001

Anonymous, *Twelve Steps and Twelve Traditions*, Alcoholics Anonymous World Services, New York  2011

Capra, Fritjof  *The Tao of Physics*, Bantam Books Inc., New York 1977

Huang, Alfred *The Complete I Ching*, Inner Traditions, Rochester, Vermont 2004

Tsu Lao  Kwok, Man-Ho; Palmer, Martin; Ramsay, Jay (editors/translators) *Tao Te Ching*, Element Books Ltd., Rockport, Mass. 1993

Wallace, David *Infinite Jest*, Little Brown and Co., Boston 1996

PROCEEDING HUMBLY

Made in the USA
Lexington, KY
23 November 2015